Bristol Banner Books

Sober Hours of Day

& The Fifth Virgin

Two-Volumes-in-One of Collected Poems

Mary Keelan Meisel

Wyndham Hall Press

SOBER HOURS OF DAY & THE FIFTH VIRGIN
Two–Volumes–in–One of Collected Poems
by Mary Keelan Meisel
(1889 - 1965)

Works by the author now available:

Children of Dusk
Vistas for Age
Sober Hours of Day
The Fifth Virgin

Works by the author in progress:

On Quiet Wings
Broken Cedar
Reins of Far Lands
Wind Among the Cedars
This Secret Ground
Paler Suns
The Bend in the Road
In Lyric Mood
Hedge Choristers
Moments of Vision
The Recluse Heart
Where Beauty Bannered

Library of Congress Catalog Card Number
89-040208

ISBN 1-55605-075-5 (paperback)

AMDG
in memorium

Mary Keelan Meisel
1889-1965

Sober Hours of Day

Mary Keelan Meisel

CONTENTS

INCOMPATIBLE

You would live, I suppose in a still convent close
That is squared with a rubble of stone,
But I, by the hour in the high conning tower
Of a clipper on wide waters borne.

You would shut out the sound of the world all around,
But my far seeking vision would strain
To see funnels and spars and the numberless stars
That are over the wind-rippled main.

You would seek the dim halls and the tight cloistral walls
While I need the quiet of space
Where I can look out on the rigging gear stout
And down on the great ocean's face.

My spirit must range in the distant and strange
And you must stay close to the hearth.
There is no husbandry for the soul that is free
Who was made to be lord of the earth.

HOLY DUSK

Poor townsfolk never know of night
Yet how much would they miss it,
If they could feel the sweetness
That burns in its holy dusk,
Away from all the trafficking
And all the proud illicit
Pleasuring that after all
Is only pleasure's husk.

Here, sounds are restful, waters run
In somnolescent fashion
And breezes stir the dogwood stars
And crisp the milkweed wings
And katydids monotonously
Decry the foolish passion
With which the hedonistic are
Pursuing glow-worm things.

If they who follow city streets
Could seek the hushed by-places
Where in some quiet cul-de-sac
Their journeyings would cease,
They'd lift their eyes a twilight time
To browse in far sky spaces,
And in these deep serenities
Would know a softer peace.

When nights are cool and effortless
The calm of Christ is hasting,
To still receptive spirits
In the free bestowal of
Delights the foolish cannot know
For in their mundane tasting
They miss the sweet that is
The essence of eternal love.

The eyes are deep with visioning-
The heart is soft with feeling,
And in the soul's recesses
Most exquisite hope is stirred,
And all the thoughts that shape themselves
Are reverent and revealing,
For they center on the evening star
Which is the promised Word.

VIEWPOINTS

The grey moonlight is chill tonight
Upon the garden wall;
It rifts and sifts through peachblow drifts
To make a paisley shawl.

The moon dust creeps through buds and steeps
A brew from their faint breath
And makes the shawl upon the wall
A cerement of death.

The while my soul looks on the whole
With terror and despair,
And thinks with dread that hopes are dead,
And life holds nothing fair,

The cool moonlight with gems bedight
Makes bright the garden wall-
It rifts and sifts through peachblow drifts.
And glowing diamonds fall.

The moonlight creeps through buds and steeps
Ambrosia for the soul,
Of sweet peach wine and lush moonshine,
And brimming wassail bowl.

The bosran dyes make bright the eyes
And dancing shadows play,
And on the wall the colors fall
More beautiful than day.

HEAVEN IN HIS EYES

My little one grew up too suddenly
And empty are my arms
And I have nothing but the memory
Of his soft baby charms.

But you, Dear Lady, suffered as I do.
But with a greater loss,
When from your arms the little Jesus grew
Up to a cross.

And so you sorrowed when He went away,
On His first ministry,
Because you knew He took the road that lay
Between you and the tree.

And being God, and knowing as He knew
How you would mourn
I think that often He comes back to you
An infant newly-born.

Each Christmas when the bells of Heaven ring
Hosannas for His birth,
And all the angels gather near to sing
"Peace, Peace on earth."

And so I think that even now He lies
When He would rest,
A tiny Babe with heaven in His eyes,
Upon your breast.

THE BACHELOR

I quarreled once with love and ever since
He hides himself behind the stippled prints
Of sunlight in the trees and makes of me
A target for his graceless archery.

He pricks me with the poisoned darts he loves-
And makes my heart a dove-cote without doves,
That, questing goes where comeliness may be-
But love's divertisements are not for me

A fowler, I who has a snare of gold,
But never captive, does my mesh enfold;
The singing birds break through my gilded net,
And spring the trap some other hand has set.

My arms are empty when they would be filled,
And love's young ardor prematurely chilled,
For all the lovely ladies that I meet,
When I advance disdainfully retreat.

My heart is ashes when abroad I go,
And damsels fair are walking to and fro,
I fall in love with each - why shouldn't I
When love is aiming at me on the sly.

It isn't that I mind the hurt a bit;
In fact I rather like the thrill of it.
All would be well if when I would pursue,
He'd draw his bow and wound the lady too.

WOODSFOLK

I go when I can
Where my kinsfolk are hiding-
The wild forest clan
Who receive me unchiding,
The woodsfolk all know me
And never are frightened
When the evening stars show me,
Or the daystar has brightened.

There are soft gentle eyes
In unquestioning faces,
In the dusk paradise
Of the still forest places.
And here in the sway
Of a verdure-hung steeple,
I am watching the play
Of the wee sylvan people.

In the storm-blasted pine
There's a horned owl sleeping,
And the fat woodmice dine
At a safe distance keeping;
The brown of the underbrush
Sheltering and pleasant,
Hides a covey of quail
And a brilliant-plumed pheasant.

A cottontail family
Is snug in the briars,
And the starlings are tuning
Innumerable lyres,
While an old raccoon chirrs
And a tree squirrel going
Over dried chestnut burrs,
Drowns an old woodcock's blowing.

The frog chug-a-rums
And a great toad is grumbling
To the pheasant's loud hums,
And the belted bees bumbling.
The trees are a-swing
With excitement of feathers,
"The year's at the spring,"
In the beast of all weathers.

NO LYRIC NET

No poet yet has prisoned lovely spring,
Nor phrasing-snared the morning talk of birds;
No lyric net has held the songs they sing,
Nor has spring's ecstacies been fleshed in words
That are so pitifully weak and few,
They cannot make its beauties flame anew.

A phrase may bring the magic back again
If ever spring has held the soul in thrall,
But passing on the witchery is vain
If one has never seen a gold spray fall
As evanescent as a dryad's sigh
Against the ephemeral wonder of the sky.

Spring has too many graces that are kin
To the unfretted gossamers of dawn;
Too fleeting to imprison them within
The meager measures that we dote upon.
Hers is the fragile loveliness that flees
Rebirth in rhymes and rhythms such as these.

VISIONS

I sing of visions that remain
Within the mystery of the brain;
Exciting fancies - rhapsodies of light.
When, commonplaces lost to view
We look upon the fairy dew
That colors all the world with new
And infinite delight.

A blessed place where one may be
Lost in a world of fantasy
When night without, is a mid-winter snare;
A mimic land of fair design,
Where rainbow threads of brilliance twine
Into a pattern that is fine
And delicate and rare.

So in this place of make-believe,
I, dreaming too, may often weave
Rich samite cloths and tapestries of dreams,
Too frail to suffer human touch;
Too beautiful for earth and much
Too fleeting for the sordid touch
Or garish morning gleams.

Then thank God for the fragile things,
And fancy's lovely whimsy wings,
When gloom would harry loneliness of mind,
How good to know the soul is free
To wander whither it would be
To glory in the legacy
That helps it seek its kind.

GOING AWAY

Go if you have to, but don't think that I
Shall care in the least. (Gee, I hope I don't cry.)

There are ever so many nice girls that I know
And most any of them would be glad if you go.

(Gosh! I hadn't thought! Just supposin that she
Will find some one else she likes better than me.)

Gosh all fishhooks, Dee Dee, why can't you stay?
There's no earthly sense in your going away.

And out to the desert! Just think of the loads
Of tarantulas and lizards and rattlers and toads,

And scorpions and gila monsters and ants,
That crawl and have wings and - Good Grief, a swell chance

You'll have to enjoy yourself out in the dumps
Where there's nothing but mesquite and cactus and stumps,

And sagebrush and centipedes, horned owls and things
With creepers and feelers and armor and stings.

Gosh! Dee Dee, you never could stand it out there.
Oh, Shucks, if you must, go and see if I care.

Girls are mostly a pain in the neck, anyway.
Gee! Gosh! It'll be lonesome with Dee Dee away.

A PRIEST FOREVER

As on the wilderness the manna fell,
So on this chosen one it falls today,
And his, the power, through God to roll away
The barrier heavens to make Love visible.
So, wistful, at the altar place he stands,
With grave young eyes in reverential awe
And marvels at the working of the law
That turns the Host to Glory in his hands.

Ordained to serve, and none more blessed that he
Who chose perfection with its cross and crown.
His is the flame that brings the Manna down
To feed the hungered with Infinity.
Another Christ! Where there is so much need-
A priest forever to bless, console and plead.

PURGATORIO

I am a sinful child, My Father. I
Fear very much that when I come to die,
I shall be halted at the Holy Place
By Cherubin who stand before Your face,
And they will chide me gently and will say,
"Because you sinned we cannot let you stay."
And I in very shame will turn away.

But there will come a pitying One to me,
To take my hand and lead me to the Tree,
Reproaching sweetly, "Child, Look on this riven
And sinless One if you would be forgiven.
Grieve for His shame who hangs there, up above,
And begs heart-service, pleading for your love,
That put Him here, a sacrificial Dove."

And looking at His face, and seeing there
The Ultima Thule, The First and Only Fair,
I shall be filled with a consuming fire;
I shall be all outpouring and desire,
And in a flame of sorrow I shall be
From all banalities of earth set free,
And all its sinfulness shall drop from me.

Some laugh and say there is no purging place.
But guilt can never look on Virtue's face,
And one who knows not Love's supernal sweet,
Must come to find it at Love's riven feet,
And seeking there a solace for his tears,
This Laodicean of the wasted years,
Must go with Mary to the place of tears.

DESPAIR

There is a strangeness in this place. It seems
An unfamiliar spirit land of dreams,
Lit with a slumbrous moon. Cold shadows lie
Beneath a line of cypresses, and nigh
The dark hill slope, a muddy river flows
Towards a molten sea. A whisper goes
Like predatory winds along its course
To chill the air from its unholy source.

"Life," so it says, "Is like this murky flow;
An instant lighted by the afterglow,
But dangerous with shoals and rotting ships,
And mud-flats where the sinuous current slips."
And then a wind-flaw ruffles the dun skies,
And weighted bitterness upon me lies,
And leaden as the waters is my mind,
That cannot run and leave this death behind.

This is not life that makes the timid shiver,
Life is not poisonous as this dank river,
Nor torn by snags nor prisoned in the shallows,
And rotting ships do not become a gallows
On which it well may choke. This is Despair
That wafts its fetid whisper on the air,
And holds me here, transfixed beyond belief,
Bound in a vast infinity of grief.

And while I wait, imprisoned in this dread,
Pure waters race across a watershed
To inundate the cypresses and sweep
The river's debris out into the deep,
And crystal clear in an exhaustless flood
It rids the stream of rotting ships and mud,
And in the silver moon swath Hope soon walks
Amid the lily pads and tule stalks.

ORDINATION

Long-looked-for day!
Long hungered-after bliss!
When Shaped-from-clay
Is vouchsafed joy like this.

The Bishop's hand
On this unworthy head!
The Lord's command,
"Make consecrate this bread."

Accomplished fact-
The lovely dream of years
The Holy Pact,
Signed with the salt of tears.

A priest at last,
By Orders set apart.
The soft ways past
And God within his heart.

GOD'S MARCHING MEN

A valiant group, a saintly troop
Comes marching down the years.
Their thunderous tread has banished dread;
Evaporated fears.

They are God's own. Before His throne
They mobilize today;
God's marching men - they come again
To help us win the fray.

The martyrs sound, "Stand! Stand your ground.
Pain vanquishes the flying.
See! Our brigade has been arrayed
In the color of our dying."

The virgins tell of convent call,
And spiritual treasures,
While foolish men were moved again
To seek their mundane pleasures.

Confessors old their lives unfold,
And learned Doctors tell
How their brigade with Jesus' aid
Had fought the good fight well.

Each trooper bears his musket, "Prayers,"
His haversack of alms.
The drummers beat, "There's no retreat.
The victor gets the palms."

Then you, who rest, rise to the test;
God's marching men appear.
Fall each in line behind the sign,
Through which they conquered fear.

The holy sign of Constantine;
The one the Crusades bore.
God's marching men must march again,
To lead us out of war.

SOBER HOURS OF DAY

Pray tell me who you are,
Who nightly comes to tease me,
When maidens, near and far,
Have ever failed to please me.

Your eyes are deep as love;
Your lips are scented fire;
Your voice that shames the dove,
Is secret as desire.

And nothing seems worth while,
That happens anywhere,
But the drama of your smile,
And the rondeau of your hair.

Why is it that you walk
So often in my sleep,
While slowly round the clock
Enchanted hours creep?

You come in trysting then
With kisses on your lips,
And we go down the glen
In little leaps and skips.

In gay and youthful joy
We romp away the hours;
A maiden and a boy
Among the blue moon flowers.

In comradeship, so sweet
The very air is stirred,
And lovely nights repeat
Each precious jewelled word.

Why must the dawning day
As though it were a blight,
Send you in haste away,
Dear Maiden of the night?

Ecstatic haunting dream
Of repetitious play,
Could you perhaps redeem
The sober hours of day?

HEROES OF GOD

I am not one with the timbre of saints
For pain is a burden I bear
With a mien that is harried and with weeping and plaints,
And a martyr-like disordered air.

O nothing is hidden that pity may gaze
For pity is pleasant to feel,
So moaning I go through the length of my days
Quite often forgetting to kneel

Like the heroes of God at the feet of the King
Who shows them that pain is a crown
And who taught them by precept and practice to fling
The burden of pleasuring down,

And to take up the cross as a cheerful release
From the travail of worldly allure,
For he tells me, like them, I will only find peace
When I have learned how to endure.

But how can I travel along with the saints
When pain is a burden I bear,
With mien that is harried and weepings and plaints
And a disordered, martyr-like air.

THE ANCHORET

As an anchoret does in a hidden wild wood,
I would lay myself down in the grasses,
And drink deepest draughts of the night's solitude,
While the moon's satin-soft garment passes

Back and forth on my brow in the lingering sweep
Of a loved lady's lovely long fingers,
And mesmerized then, I would settle to sleep,
To the song of the forest's night singers.

And no repercussions from noisier worlds
Would ever encroach on my slumbers;
Except the slow drop of invisible pearls
In constantly augmented numbers,

Would sound in the balconied courts of the night
In the cool of the green forest clearing
And I would awake to ephemeral light
With expectancy sharpening hearing.

And over my head on the fringe of the trees,
Where the fronds of the treetops are swaying,
So faint, it would seem like the murmur of bees,
I would hear a vast multitude praying.

There would come to my ears in this buttressed old wood
Ere the early dawn's new-painted glowing,
The prayers of the hermits who found living good
In this place beyond sinful world's knowing.

And there with the anchorets kneeling in prayer
My soul would expand to desire
While the night candles dimmed in the sweet scented air,
And the Daystar rose higher and higher.

YOUTHFUL MOTHER

What is in your youthful mind,
Unfledged and untried mother,
Sedately walking through the park,
While pushing it before,
The gray gondola carriage
Where is sleeping now, no other
Than the little child that sprang from you
And you but scarcely more?

Newly-fashioned Motherkin,
Is life for you a doll house?
And love a youngster's plaything too,
That you may tire of?
Or has your wee one made you see
How much it means, the small house
That pivots all your little world,
And centers all your love?

Are visions in your restless mind,
Small immature Madonna,
Or can you see the great man now
That your wee son might be?
Then for his future crowning weave
For him a pure corona,
And wear it always on your brow
That his young eyes may see.

That when the fruitful years are done
And vision fructifying,
You too, may sing "Magnificat"
As did a Mother-maid,
And your tall son will rise up too,
And bless with love undying
The young and lovely mother who
Faced living unafraid.

LOVE PROMISES SO MUCH

Love promises so much and can fulfill
So little, so you say who do not know
What love is like and how its ardors spill
Into a waiting heart to make it grow
Like to itself. Pure, crystalline and still
Becomes a life that feels the overflow
Of sweetness that is love which grows until
The earth is lit with all its inner glow.

This much love can fulfill and does for those
Who open wide their hearts to let Him in
To drive therefrom all wickedness and sin
And leave instead an infinite repose.
Peace deep and calm and sweet is their reward
Who are fulfilled in Him their loving Lord.

WHAT PRICE BEAUTY

Apologies to J. U. Nicholson

Queen Nefert lived in Egypt some four thousand years ago,
And if you asked who Nefert was not many men would know
And yet they called her beautiful, and made her live in stone;
In lovely statuettes and busts her pulchritude was shown.

And there were geniuses who carved the lady's stately grace,
And gemmed the frieze of palace walls with profiles of her
     face,
And many fine inscriptions were unearthed along the Nile
That praised Queen Nefert's beauty and the charm of Nefert's
     smile.

But what of lovely ladies that are dust four thousand years?
And what of ancient geniuses who carved the ladies' ears?
Sarcophagi and sacred urns and Tel-el-Amarna's past
Are nothing but the charrings from an age that did not last.

And only archaeologists are charmed with what they know
Of all the lovely ladies that have lived so long ago.
For beauty dead has no appeal, and Neferts that have been
Have been eclipsed a million ways by sirens of the screen.

Slim-contoured girls, firm-fleshed and fleet - we see them
     everywhere,
We're surfeited with beauty and we're bored with ladies fair.
But when four thousand years have gone will excavators find
The face that launched a thousand films, for which ten thou-
     sand pined?

The sweethearts of the T.V. screens; curvaceous cover girls;
The cigarette ad darlings and chorines who marry earls-
Will these from ancient magazines smile at a future age,
In luscious toothsome loveliness from every faded page?

STRAUSS OF THE GOLDEN GATE

They walk across, an endless multitude
That asks not whence it rose nor whose the brain
That from impenetrable mists had wooed
These strands across the straits and back again,
To mesh the sun and hold the flame of rain.

A score of years' devotion to one thought;
Long vigils when the fire of genius burned;
A dedication that in silence wrought;
And all the littleness of living spurned
To make the masterpiece for which he yearned.

He shaped his thoughts to greatness as he spun
His dreams across this spider-web of space:
A golden web of promise that would run
In threads of commerce, gossamer as lace,
And etched in beauty on the sunset's face.

Spume flashed and currents dove beyond the strait,
And troughs spilled water to the waiting sea,
But he drove on and bridged the Golden Gate
With loveliness that none had dreamed could be,
A miracle above immensity.

Strauss of the Golden Gate! Whose genius flung
The Bridge across the millrace of the tide.
Strauss who had dreamed of beauty and then hung
A masterpiece upon the oceanside
Sing out his name and shout it far and wide.

TWILIGHT SMOKE

There was a cleric's robe-
A cope of cloth-of-gold
Beneath a crystal globe
With lamp flames in its heart.
A wind from out the sea,
Came tearing it apart,
Till, riven suddenly,
It spun out, fold on fold.

Their golden fringes sprayed
Swept by the sea-shot wind,
Upon the sprinkling sea
Like tatters of brocade,
And needles of the spray
Caught up the bands and pinned
Them web-like on the way
Where soon the sun would be.

Descending low, it tore
Through interlacing cloth,
And spun about the core
Until the crystal broke,
And combers doused the flames
Within their sizzling froth,
Till sea and sky became
A purple twilight smoke.

MAY BRINGS YOU BACK

May brings you back, and I am quite content
To have you go when May herself has gone.
Were you to longer stay, rememberance spent
Of its stored sweetness would go on and on
Through wearying sequences until the past
Would crush me with the old wild grief at last.

And so when you return each shining May,
The cooling blood to quickening rhythms speeds,
And I can live again each lovely day
In certain knowledge that while memory feeds
Upon the blissful hours I shall remain
Impervious to youth's bewildering pain.

For all the golden days of May are sweet,
With promises and dreams and we may walk
The memoried graceful paths with eager feet,
And let delight renew itself in talk
As pleasantly and sweet as is the breeze,
That curls itself within the burgeoned trees.

May holds a benediction for the heart,
That moves serenely through its fragrant bowers,
And so we meet again who have to part,
And find the joy we lost in April's showers.
Yet I am quite content that May is brief,
And much too beautiful to harbor grief.

EACH IN HIS TURN

Each in his turn drops to his final place,
And dust fills up the hollows of his face.
Each in his turn lies in his narrow bed,
Supine at length, the restless spirit fled.

And from each death a newer life will grow,
And blood congealed will make new sap to flow,
So he, who dying gloriously goes
To tint a peach or glorify a rose.

And sometimes from the place where spirits go,
A vapory form may come and hover low,
And say, "This flower that is so lovely now
Was once the smooth white polish of my brow;

And this rose that with languorous sweetness drips
Was once the perfect lacquer of my lips;
(One said that they were fair), and this slim tree
Grew straight and tall because it grew from me.

Yes, It was good to live - and good to die,
Since I live doubly, here and in the sky,
Whose soul untrammeled took the fleeing mind
Aloft on prayer and left the flesh behind.

And I who knew but oneness now am two,
The soul that soars with God - this life with you:
Blessed in a dual immortality-
This I that am and this that sprang from me.

MILDRED DORAN

Into the west on the pinions of air,
A gallant young woman went flying.
We watched her go out with a tear and a prayer,
But none saw her fall and no one could tell where,
Nor know of the way of her dying.

Dauntless young Mildred with stars in her eyes,
Gay-hearted and high-strung and daring,
Dreamed of the islands and reached for the prize,
And journeyed afar into alien skies
Unfriendly as yet to such faring.

True to her forebears - a Gael of the Gaels
She went where the Trade Winds were blowing,
Disdaining the earth and abandoning sails,
She followed the lure of the undefined trails,
Her back to the easy ways going.

Frail was the ship and uncertain the day,
And the fog hid the dangerous waters,
But the plane rose in beauty above the still bay,
Like a cloud-ship it lifted and hurried away,
With one of earth's loveliest daughters.

We saw her go out in a last gallant fling,
Where the Farralone's light-ships were lying,
And feared for the message the morning would bring,
And the waste of wild waters that reached for the wing
Of the monoplane that she was flying.

And then followed silence, abysmal and deep,
And the straining of hearts unto breaking,
And we knew not the secret the waters would keep,
Nor the place where the lovely young Mildred would sleep,
At the end of her brave undertaking.

The air-trek was over and poignantly then
We thought of the spirited flier,
With borrowed wings clipped and the courage of ten,
Who dropped to her death with a silent "Amen,"
And a soul of unconquerable fire.

EUCALYPTUS GROVES

I think that were elves in droves
Within the park last night,
Because the eucalyptus groves
At dawn were covered quite
With the perky tams the wee folk wear,
And red cockades were everywhere.

But something must have halted play
Last night within the glade,
To frighten the small men away
To seek the deeper shade,
For they incontinently flew
In panic from their rendezvous.

A rakish set these little men
Who hide away at noon
Will gambol over moor and glen
When there's a summer moon,
The while the gauzy moonlight flows
On cambric shirt and motley hose.

To lonely glen and coppice green
They hie away at dawn
But they are shifting shadows seen
On night's spot-lighted lawn,
When moonlight pours its silver tide
Upon them as they dip and glide.

Tip-tilted shoes and dockades spin
And coat-tails whirl as they begin
Till doffing waistcoats and cockades
They toss them in the forest glades
And foot the dance to fairy tune
With tricksy lilt of scarlet shoon.

And gay and wild their measures beat,
And faster go their dancing feet,
And fast and faster do they swing
Within the night's enchanted ring,
Until their tams of thimble size
Drop rakishly athwart their eyes.

And these upon the greensward lay
When sunlight pierced the trees,
Proclaiming to the coming day
The night's festivities,
When elfin men with dancing feet
Tripped to a measure fast and sweet.

HIBISCUS

One, at the sunset hour,
Came saying, "Lani, wear
This fair hibiscus flower
In your lovely dusky hair.

And when the noon of night,
Cajoles the lover's moon
To shower hoarded light
On canna and lagoon,

I'll come and know you then
By the flower in your hair,
For, Lani, to all men
Every dusky maid is fair

When the moonlight dowers all
With her witchery and grace,
And I would but forestall
Another haunting face

From slipping in with lures
To the pledging of my mind,
When my heart is only yours
And your heart is ever kind.

There is room for no one there
With your gentle starshine power,
So, Lani, in your hair,
Wear this sweet hibiscus flower."

And so when night dipped down
And moonshine lit the sea,
The lover came from town
To where his Love would be.

And everywhere were maids
As lovely as the night,
With dusky tresses sprayed
With hibiscus blossoms bright,

And all along the shore
Were maids to light the gloom
And every dark head wore
A great hibiscus bloom.

And since then island girls,
Made conscious of its power
Have decked their dusky curls
With a great hibiscus flower.

HAPLESS FOLK

In sunless caves and windless seas
From here to the antipodes,
Who dwell?
Who can tell
If hapless folk are toiling yet-
Unlucky gnomes who moil and sweat
With days a groan and nights, a fret;
Doomed so to spend
In unremitting never-end
Their cursed existance underground.
Has no one found
The evidence that old tales lie-
That some were born who will not die-
Wee hapless folk of monstrous shapes,
Who live where never sound escapes,
In grottos dank and caverns chill,
Where subterranean rivers spill;
Where stalagmites and stalagtites
Are pointing through the endless nights.

If such there be, then who are they,
These creatures whom the old men say,
Were stopped upon their heedless way
As they incontinently fell
From Paradise to people Hell?
Are Queen Titania and Puck
And Ariel the brands whose luck
Found them on earth as that was said
That stopped them as they downward sped
In answer to Saint Michael's plea:
"Where they are now, Lord, let them be."

And if these tales told long ago,
By wise old men are truly so,
How just and proper they should hide
These fallen angels doomed by pride
In bracken, coppice, brake and glen
A warning to pride-swollen men.
And yet for them God's mercy spoke
And their unholy journey broke
Just short of that accursed spot
Where Beelzebub and Satan plot
New tortures for the sad ingrate
For whom Saint Michael spoke too late.

WE CLIMBED THE HILL

We climbed the hill we two, when we were young,
So many times, for we were fond of climbing,
And as we panted to the top we clung
Each to the other. Then the sunset lining
The hills beyond made us seem close and cherished,
So lovely did it seem at the day's close
And when the colors with their beauty perished
We watched a while until the moon arose.

And in its glow we dropped down from the hill
Thoughtful at length because the day had ended
And night had come and all the world was still
And we were by Infinity attended.
One has to love to feel as we did then
Stirred to the depths by what God gives to men.

THE SEA-GIRT LAND

August, in hinterland places is shimmering heat on the land,
And vibrating heat-waves whose rhythm is bond to the dry
    stirless grass;
But here it is cool with the sea wind, that billowing over the
    sand
Is bearing the breath of the ocean wherever the gray fogs
    must pass.

It is the surge of the tide where the stripped eucalyptus is
    holding
Its billows of greenery so low that its peeled trunk is swept as
    with spray;
It is the ebbing of waves in the dense cryptomeria folding
Their grasping and gainless sharp fingers to keep it from slip-
    ping away.

It is the foam that had birth in the caves that the sea-urchins
    cherish,
Keeping a tryst with the town in the sombering hush of the
    night;
It is a ghostly white galleon that fated forever to perish,
Is full-rigged and still under way crowned ever with St. Elmo's
    light.

Here is the langurous land that is tented with fog in midsummer,
Dreams are as soft as the mist that is curtaining sea-scape
    and sky;
Lotus-land, girt by the sea, it is never disturbed by the drummer
That walks in the pageant of Time, and beats as the hours go by.

I SHALL ARISE AGAIN

I shall arise again. I was not made
To lie in this chill grave and rot away.
This pallid perishable thing you laid
So gently here is but a bit of clay
That held its moulded form as long as I
Had life within and would not let it die.

And I shall rise again. This much I know:
I am invincible against decay.
This body that encased me once may blow
As dust motes on the air and float away.
What matters it? The spirit that is I
Is winged for spaces out beyond the sky.

I shall arise again. One rose before,
And conquered death with splendor on His face,
And my dissevered being shall once more
Be one again in His immortal place,
So till the trumpet of that day is sounded,
What matters that by which I am surrounded.

For I shall rise again and these earth-born
And utterly repugnant clothes of Time
Shall on the ring of resurrection morn
Be reassambled from the tombs green slime
And being re-united with its soul
Become an archangelic-radiant whole.

THE WORLD FORGETS

The world forgets its heroes all too soon.
The furor caused by fame dies quickly down;
And he who went a conquering king at noon,
At midnight sees another wear his crown.

A little hour when tumult shouts his name;
When nations pause to give their meed of praise,
And then no one has care from whence he came,
Nor how nor where he spends his later days.

The adulation of the multitude
Meant naught to you, Amundsen, towards the end,
When with your back against the wall you stood,
Alone, who once called every man your friend.

The frigid land you conquered was less cold
Than shoulders turned when your brief hour was past,
And you were glad I think to feel the fold
Of its chill hand about your heart at last.

Take courage, Lindberg, too, for genius pays
The price of greatness in a world apart,
Because you could not walk the beaten ways,
They took the thorns and pressed them to your heart.

Processionals of triumph: pageantries
Where mania flings palm branches down the way,
Napoleon knew; Columbus, Socrates,
And saw with you their glory rot away.

The world forgets the heroes and their deeds.
Hysteria gone; its fitful fever, ash.
It scourges him who for his vision bleeds,
And scornfully lays on his back, the lash.

The world forgets them, but their name endures,
Emblazoned on the pages of the years,
For History to record, and Lindberg, yours
Grows brighter through the clarity of tears.

THE CHILDREN'S LIBRARY

A wide pleasant room where the morning sun enters,
In six double panes and lies thick on the floor,
Where eager big sisters are acting as mentors,
To borrowers crowding the desk and the door.

Tables as round as King Arthur's are ranging
With comradely chairs where the book shelvings go,
And elfin-eyed children are busy exchanging
Great picture-backed books in a colorful row,

And dreamy-eyed children are turning the pages
Of buckram-bound wisdom, and hunting its lore;
And they who are done with their poets and sages
Are turning their books in and asking for more.

The tiniest tables are down in the corner,
Where big-lettered cloth-bounds with gay painted backs
Show Hi-Diddle-Diddle and little Jack Horner,
And the cow that goes "Moo," and the duckling that quacks.

The tops of the book shelves are gay with narcissi,
And Red Riding Hood meets the wolf on the wall,
And a yellow-skinned mite and an almond-eyed missy,
Are intrigued with the painting of Jack and Jill's fall.

The middle-sized tables are up in the center,
Where twelve year olds gather to thrill to romance,
And read of great castles where courtiers enter
And curtsy and dip to the throb of the dance.

Sophisticate teens tread the book aisles unheeding
The wee and engrossed ones at tables and chairs;
Secure in their wisdom, mature in their reading,
They look the shelves over and choose of its wares.

Book stalls before which desire walks slowly,
As though by some legerdemain it could see,
Materialized there all the great and the lowly
That crowd the bound pages and are waiting to be.

STERLING

Poor Sterling! On whose genius tarnished fingers
Traced talon-like, the sullen scroll of death!
Across your amaranthined tomb there lingers
The blemish of the hen-bane's poisoned breath.

And those you left behind can only censure
The way you took for you were proud and strong,
And should have waited for the great adventure
To leave unsullied your bequest of song.

But hurrying your life away from duty,
You lost the precious heritage of Time,
Unravelling the harmonies of beauty
That you had woven into deathless rhyme.

And now your songs have lost the breathless magic
Unsullied genius gives and small frail ghosts,
They grope at midnight questioning and tragic,
Pale visions born of fragile empty boasts.

One looked for more in one so nobly gifted;
Who had so much to compensate for pain.
Could you have come from suffering, uplifted,
At one with Him who makes the rough ways plain.

Your wounds would grow to newer understanding,
Since flesh must swoon to pain and tears must flow,
And all must yield their bodies to the branding,
And find their strength in knowing this is so.

We cannot know the urge for dissolution
Your troubled spirit knew. We only feel
Tormented sorrow at the execution
Of genius before life unwound its reel.

The life that made you vocal should have lengthened
To fruitful years. You had no right to go,
Self-ushered, Friend, Your sorrow should have strengthened
The art you loved. There is a need for woe.

CONTINUITY

All the movements in this place,
Never noticed I
Until, one evening, conquering haste,
I lay me down to die.

All the movements day by day,
Mostly made by me,
When upon my back I lay,
Did not cease to be.

So, detached, I lay and heard
All the busy sounds
That about the house occured,
And about the grounds.

Where were other workers' treads
Where my footsteps stopped.
Some one else picked up the threads
That my fingers dropped.

So 'twas borne upon me then,
Lying sick-a-bed,
There will be no difference when
I am lying dead.

When my active hours are run,
And is chilled my heart,
All my labor, left undone,
Some one else will start.

Lying there I seemed to see
All the years ahead,
When the one that follows me
Will be lying dead.

And these others would pursue
Duties they had left.
They would be as eager too,
Willing, quick and deft.

Down through time successively
Each would follow after,
Passing on the legacy
Of living with its laughter.

So the race unbrokenly
To Time's ending flows.
I or some one else like me
In moving drama goes.

FROM A CASEMENT

I have looked down at life from a high casement seat,
That was cushioned as deeply as window-seats are,
And saw the dawns burning and hot suns retreat,
And crescents dim down to a star.

I have watched the bewildering flux and the flow
Of the currents of life shuttling by,
And noted how traffic ran swiftly below,
Or rocketed into the sky.

I have sat like the Lady of storied Shallot,
A witness with eyes bearing down
On those who were feted and those who had fought
Or were loved in the brilliant white town.

And away from the turmoil, I've sat and I've gazed
And wondered and gazed down again,
And there on the borderland, shocked and amazed,
I have thought of the strange ways of men.

They cry out, "Peace, Peace!" And there never is peace
And their clamor is harsh to the ear;
And the sound of their bickering never does cease,
And their words are offensive to hear.

I have sat above all of the turmoil and fret,
From dark to the flaming of dawn,
And marveled how often the foolish forget
The troubles their rancor bring on.

The orbits of those who are passing below
Do not touch even lightly my own,
But I cannot forget though detached from their woe,
How the seeds of their sorrows are sown.

And I wish they could stand in a high place apart,
And dwell on the fruits of their pride,
And then they would know that peace comes to the heart,
When Humility walks by their side.

CHOICE

There is a lover for whom I have thoughts
That are always so precious and tender,
Since I have been shaken with knowing how great
And desperate his need is of me;
And there is another for whom my heart beats
In a constant and gallant surrender
So that it would lie in his keeping as still
As a gull in the trough of the sea.

Sometimes when I turn and look back at the porch
Where the portico vines have nigh hidden
My passing from them and I peep at the place
Where my lovers impatiently wait,
And at sight of the one there are tears that are hot,
And that rise up unchecked and unbidden,
But my heart, recognizing the other calls out
Most imperiously for its mate.

And I ask myself then, "Shall I marry the one
Whose need is so obviously urgent,
And how shall I stand to look into his eyes
If my own need should answer him nay;
And should I in pity say yes to his plea
Would my heart, dispossessed and insurgent
Go out in despair in quick search of the mate
It had desperately driven away?"

SINCE YOU WENT HENCE

It is not quite the same since you went hence.
The birds have just a little sadder song,
And things stay somehow just where they belong,
Which is a rather new experience.

The sun has gone. Why it should go with you
Is far beyond my power to fathom, yet
A little later, I shall cease to fret
So clouds will lighten and the sun break through.

I cannot see the stars at night. They glow
No doubt as brilliantly where you are gone-
A bar is even held against the dawn
So no exquisite sunrise tints may show.

Dear little Boy, grown tall, how foolishly
I weep because you have been called away,
And years are broken and the skies are gray,
And memories are crushing ceaselessly.

Soon I shall gather all the things you left,
And fold them all away, so close, so dear,
And turn myself to face the coming year,
And smile down on my heart that is bereft.

A mother grasps in vain the broken years,
For youth must go to that which youth must do,
And though I grieve I cannot hinder you,
My loved and lost one by these foolish tears,

So I shall fret for just a little while
While you go on to your appointed task,
And I shall weave new years behind the mask
That I shall wear with such a gentle smile.

TO EVERY HAPPY THOUGHT

Romanticists have told their tales of love,
And poets have grown rapturous with words
In praise of it, and lovers dreaming of
Its sweet fulfillment hear the songs of birds
And the enchantment of a moonlit sky,
When love is mentioned and they are bewitched
By circean magic or a lovelit eye
That may or may not make their lives enriched.

I find that love is more than just a name-
It's easier to say what it is not
Than what it is. I know before you came
I could have taken every happy thought
And added birdsong. Now that I've lost you
To every happy thought I've added rue.

MOUNT SAINT SEPULCHRE

Dear chimes of Mount Saint Sepulchre,
I hear your sweetness thrill
Along the trembling silences
Of Calvary's tragic hill.

And hearing, I am back again,
A weeping worshipper,
Upon the mount of Mary's pain,
Where I must go with her.

And there are tears and grief in store,
For where sweet Mary trod,
Each heart must sob and sorrow for
The tragedy of God.

Matins and Lauds! Gethsemane's
Unutterable woe;
Red torches in the olive trees;
The friend become the foe.

Tierce! And the weary road alone;
With mockers on the way;
The terrors of the altar stone-
Where men have come to slay.

Compline! The flame of wounding spent;
The poor racked body still;
The heavens torn - the whole earth rent,
And darkness on the hill.

Vespers! The cool of winding sheets,
To shroud the precious dead;
The sealed tomb and the mourning seats,
And twelve uncomforted.

Dear Holy Chimes, you come to chide,
When I would reckless stray;
To bring me back to Mary's side,
To sorrow and to pray.

To make me kneel upon the ground,
And share sweet Mary's pain,
For with each blowing leaf of sound
I see a white lamb slain.

APRIL GROWN SUDDENLY DARK

Night and the stars
Serene in the beauty of space,
Dawn and the sunrise bars,
And the Daystar secure in its place.
Dawn and the dark,
And shadows and sun on the lea;
Song-soaring lark,
And gulls dipping down to the sea.

April as sweet
As ever an April gone by;
Hours as fleet
And as buoyant as clouds in the sky.
All drawing near
To the hour predestined to be,
When the Holy and Dear
Would be pinioned in shame to a tree.

Travelling on
From the Sea of Tiberius down
Through the dusk and the dawn
Through welcoming village and town.
Triumphal hours
With palm branches strewing the way;
Burgeoning flowers,
And budlets preparing for May.

Love in the hearts
Of the simple, the pure and the true
Hatred that darts
When the Sanhedrin Councils are through.
And the cross lifts him up
As the wind lifts the wings of the lark,
And leaves Him to die
In an April grown suddenly dark.

ETCHINGS

I sometimes wonder if our ways would cross,
And we should stand together in some place
Far distant from our youth would there be loss,
Revealed in gentle etchings on your face.

I think that we should feel no vague surprise
If somewhere, we could meet again, we two,
And I would glimpse the pain behind your eyes,
And you would know that I had suffered too.

Oh, I would know you better if the signs
Of suffering were there upon your face,
To match the grief on mine that penciled lines
Too deep for any unguents to erase.

BESIDE THE FIRE GLOW

The splendor of the day has dimmed;
The hours of labor passed;
The cottager, so weary-limbed
Comes home to rest at last.

He sees his lowly cot with plume
Of hearth-smoke gayly blown,
And mingled with the dogwood bloom
He smells the fresh baked pone.

The bacon sizzles and his wife
With smiling welcome turns,
And weariness is shed from life
And youthful fire burns.

No reckoning the daily grind;
The rows of corn to hoe;
All weariness is left behind
Beside the fire glow.

ACACIAS

This is the tree beneath which I could picture
Fairies at play on soft moonlighted eves,
The greensward at their dancing feet gay-stippled
With changing patterns of thin-shadowed leaves.

I must come forth some night when all is quiet-
When never a slight breeze stirs the dreaming earth,
And see if I can see the great tree's shadow
Disturbed by ecstacies of fairy mirth.

It may be I shall glimpse a pixie brogan-
Or are the wee folk barefoot when they play.
Perhaps the Little People will receive me
As kindolk when we dance the hours away.

And maybe Mab will wave a spangled star-wand,
Or Oberon sport with his immortal band,
And I shall leave the gray world and go dancing
Into the gold of an enchanted land.

Sometimes the hidden night is like a lodestone
With gay acacias rippling to sweet sound,
And then I know the fairy clans are massing
For ceremonial dancing on the ground.

At such a time there is an unease stirring
Among the grass tips in the fairy ring,
And all the overarch is liquid motion,
And fluent night is charged with reveling.

And do you think if such a night would lure me
Where the moon-arras of the tree is spread,
That all the Little Folk would keep me dancing
And Maeve would put a changeling in my bed.

PERSPECTIVES

With vision focussed on the ground,
I see distressful things:
A writhing angle-worm, half-drowned;
A house-fly's broken wings;
A wounded snail; a tarnished mound
Where rotted winter clings.

But when an impulse lifts my eyes
From sodden things below,
The rift within the sullen skies
Is like a shining bow,
And cradled there, the red sun lies,
All in a summer glow.

A HOUSE LIFTED UP

When the day is troubled
And the spirit becomes as water
Into which the juice of aloes has been stirred,
And melancholy and the desolation of doomed places
Is in your thoughts,
Come to Me,
For I have kept Myself close to you,
And I have lifted up a House
Into which you may come to find peace.

I have made My House a Tabernacle of Beauty,
For I would show unto you the solace of beauty.
You will find Me otherwhere-
In Golden Gate Park-
In Kew Gardens,
And somewhere near the Pai-Fang
Across a silver Chinese stream.
But much more will you find Me in My own House.

The wearied have been here;
The sick and the maimed have found comforting
And they that are without sight
Have been privileged to see
The ruby of the Sanctuary light
Burning behind the marble and bronze
Of the altar railing.

I have lifted up a House;
I have made It a Tabernacle of Beauty,
Of solemnity and strength;
Buttresses and pylons have added solidity
To its material structure.
But I am the Bread of Life
That am the sustenance of the Spirit,
So come to Me.

Across the Steps of Exorcism
Where you will see the pomegranate vine
Which has been made for you
The symbol of immortality.
The lillies of Sharon are here,
And roses from the same place,
And sheaves of wheat and twirlings of the grape
For here in My House will be found
Symbolism and mysticism
Which are the foods of the spirit.

Here also are rose windows and filigree traceries-
Soaring arches pointing to dim groined roofs-
Vaulted shadows and exquisite bas-reliefs
In bronze triptyches-
Heraldic colorings and mellow oaken panels
With dedicated carvings-
Multiplicities of beauties and harmonies are here,
And music is made manifest;
Nuances of light between foliations of
High clerestory windows, filtering the sunlight
Of sacramental fires;
Behind the niches of the Apse
Are the Reredos of the great altar of marble and flame;
Bronze candleabra and candlelight
Picking out threads of gold lace
On the Place of Sacrifice.

I have lifted up a House,
And I have made it beautiful and serene
And full of the promise of ultimate peace.
But most of all I have made a Place
Where I too may dwell,
For My delight has been from Eternity
To be with the children of men.

So come to Me, all you
Who are heavy-laden and lay your burdens
At My feet, in the House
Where I have so longed to dwell
With you.
Come to Me all you who labor and are sad,
And I will make you rich and happy
With the richness of My Heart
In My own House.

NEW LEISURE

I would but ask that you could share this beauty
Before whose shrine I kneel. I never knew
There was so much of loveliness when Duty
Kept me in bondage as the swift years flew.

Now I have leisure for these lovely hours,
And you are bound within a narrow room;
I walk through slanting rain and cherry showers
While hawthorns bud and rhododendrons bloom.

And feel so grieved betimes because the leaven
Of life is in the bread on which I feast,
While you who should be part of this brief heaven,
At labor, perish, Toil's accustomed Priest.

TO A HOUSE NEWLY PAINTED

Since they have painted your wide window bows,
And laid the brush on lintel, trave and sill;
Renewed your mansard with neat shingled rows,
And bronzed the interstices of your grill;

Since they have made your contours sharp and clear,
And nailed the loosened clapboards back in place,
And flagged the footpath leading to the rear,
And made the garden close a thing of grace;

Since they repaired the sagging porch and set
Pergolas at each side where roses bend,
And latticed dormers and restored the fret
And filigree about the gable's end;

Since they have made your front facade suggest
The dignity of cool wide rooms and space,
They made new beauty for the tranquil guest
To bloom from this once desolated place.

INTO SOUND AND SIGHT

In the still night I hear the sound of singing,
Borne on the air from some place far away,
Far off and sweet it bridges night while bringing
A solace to a heart no longer gay.
There is no tumult in the air around me
But in my heart it rages fierce and strong,
Probing the bitter sorrows that surround me,
And all the griefs that have remained too long.

They master pain - the gentle singing voices
That have been filtered through the waves of night,
And bring the hearthside where a group rejoices,
Out from the dark and into sound and sight.
And rusty from disuse my voice enraptured,
Lifts up to join the song the night has captured.

ROSALITA

"There's no one sweet as Rosalita"
A bird sang from a gnarled oak tree,
And looking at you, Senorita,
I could do nothing but agree.

It was a still day in September,
A Sabbath peace seemed to abide,
And nothing stirred as I remember
In all the lovely country side.

Then suddenly a bird's wolf whistle
Awoke the stillness and you stirred,
And from your lap a Sunday missal
Dropped at my feet. Oh lovely Bird!

I stooped retrieving it and passed it
To you with such a courtly bow
That I am sure you must have classed it
With your ancestral folk somehow.

At any rate you smiled as sweetly
As your great-aunt would at her Don.
I took advantage of it neatly
And dropped beside you on the lawn.

Oh Rosalita, Rosalita!
I thank that unknown bird for this.
Without his whistle, Senorita,
How much enchantment would I miss.

FIRST LINES

The Fifth Virgin

Mary Keelan Meisel

CONTENTS

THE FIFTH VIRGIN

Within the room, like Mary of Magdala,
I wait the Holy One;
With trimmed lamp and the window gleaming gaily
In the reflected sun.

How long the time when eagerness is waiting;
And the seconds, slow to pass;
The footsteps lag; the shadows press the grating;
Low grows the hourglass.

The dusk is lit; the evening star grows stronger;
Night comes with quiet art,
And apprehension lest He tarry longer
Makes cowardly my heart.

What if the hours should find my lamp grown dimmer;
The oil supply burned down
And all the stars erased; the crescent slimmer,
And darkness on the town.

And if no flame would light Him to my casement
To show Him where I wait,
How could I go in shame and self-abasement
To open the outer gate.

Lord, tarry not, but hasten to the feasting;
The banquet cloth is spread,
And all awaits the glory of Your priesting;
The breaking of the Bread.

Lord, hasten where Your little handmaid lingers
Within the room apart,
With lamp held high in white and trembling fingers
That would betray her heart.

I WALK WITH THOUGHTS

I walk with thoughts immense as is the daystar,
I dream great visions, deeper than is space,
My stature is the hill that hides yon chaste star,
Yet I am circumscribed in this small space.

Though I am bound to this grim wheel of labor
To grind the pabulum the frail flesh needs,
My soul can climb the stars, or kneel on Tabor,
It does not fail because the body bleeds.

STRONG WINGS

Strong wings that bear in restless lines, across the windy sky,
Did I not see the idling air, scarce stirred by your slow flight
A few noons back, and now, today, like frenzied moths you fly
And weave about through tortured clouds, battalions of fright.

Calm motifs on the azure sky, you rode the seas of summer;
Gaunt black, you beat the ceiling now, so gray instead of blue-
Like shadows on the shadowed air, both early and late comer,
Are driven by encroaching storms, that closely follow you.

Now blown like leaves before the wind, storm signals rushing
    forward,
With tattered refugees of clouds, consorting with grim fear,
You leave behind the turmoil of the winds that ravish shore-
    ward,
And lift the wide gray waters to belabour mole and pier.

Haunted, apprehensive wings, stampeded with the knowing
That stalking them unweariedly is the unuttered word,
And yet, despite the bellows of the wind with certain going,
They win the blessed inland refuge of the hunted bird.

THE AIR IS FULL OF WINGS

The air is full of wings today,
Clouds cobble the low sky.
The sea's horizon bears away
Where wan veiled billows lie,
And whitecaps dart beyond the gray
Fog gauze that shudders by.

One need not say why restless wings
Are flurrying the air-
A wedge along the shoreline brings
A breath from otherwhere,
And gulls and blackbirds pattern wings
As wild geese southward bear.

Tireless wings of migrant flocks
In swift and steady flight
Above the guanoed harbor rocks
Lay out a trail of light,
With shining goal the slim reed stalks
That swing in tropic bight.

Above the wall and hummocked sands,
The shore birds, mewing wheel,
And refugees from frozen lands
Disdaining snipe and teal,
Swing south in straight converging bands,
On pinions strong as steel.

THE LAST SWALLOW

For the last swallow flying to the south,
There is no need to grieve, yet nonetheless
I stand and gaze, my hand across my mouth
Lest I cry out in utter loneliness.

In this dispassionate and cold gray land
I feel frigidity of soul when they,
His kinsfolk, with retiring wings have fanned
Our hostile air. I follow on the way,

To trail the voyagers with hungry dreams
To that warm isle where they will come to rest,
Bend with the pampas grass above the streams
Beside which they will end their splendid quest.

I shatter distance when along the sky
I bear the last lone migrant on his way,
But when the light absorbs him, how can I
Turn back to face the disappointing day.

But He who makes the air a highway for
The tiny creatures who must flee the cold,
Must give me strength to stand this frozen shore
That clutches me and loosens not its hold.

They flee the winter with its stormy woe,
But I must try my soul with dread and fear,
And loneliness and grief. I cannot go
Till I have proved myself by staying here.

REPETITION

He drives the cows today
Along the sunny lane
Where yesterday there moved
Another lowing train,
And dust of many hooves
Rolled upward from the plain.

And you would see, were you
To live a trillion moons,
Another drover's herd
Move to his whistled tunes
Out to the pasture lands
To browse in sultry noons.

And would you live beyond
The space of millions more,
You'd hear the herd boy's call,
And see him at his chore
Of driving lowing kine,
With driving stick before.

Be heavens gray or blue-
The place without a name,
The dream repeats itself;
The picture is the same-
The moving kine and boy,
And peace within the frame.

GOTHIC

I would my soul were a cathedral place
Of stained glass beauty and of soaring prayer,
That swings above life's nave and into space
As Gothic arches seek the upper air.

I would that life would buttress my desires
And fling the vaults of aspiration high,
And rear facades that terminate in spires
With golden crosses on the crimson sky.

I would that choir and transept, apse and aisle,
Would beautifully sweep in rhythmic lines,
Of rectitude, sans worldliness and guile,
With traceries of truth in rich designs.

I would that on the altar of my heart,
The Infinite could come at least to rest,
And find therein its humble counterpart,
And be therein a most beloved guest.

INDIVIDUALISTS

A wall of fog that holds the threat of rain;
By winds of ocean torn;
And seabirds cutting through the misty plain
On strong wings, inland borne.
A gust of gulls; a fret of swallow wings
That whip a sky, no longer morning-blue;
All driving eastward as the tempest flings-
All but a laggard few.
What folly is it goads them forth and back
Through tattered fog and tempest driven wrack!

Is it grim fear, or foolish zest that drives
Them through the danger zone,
To risk their so inconsequential lives
In folly, vagrant-blown?
When all their fellows take the sea-wind's road
To hinterlands where refuges are warm,
How is it that these few feel not the goad
Of the approaching storm,
And, individualists, refuse to follow
The flight of gull or inland trek of swallow?

Are they of those who will not go along
When fearful captains lead,
But, who, unconscious of the fleeing throng-
An ampler-visioned breed-
See panic, greed or folly whip the crowd,
And stay their flight or move the other way,
And in their calm acceptance or their proud
Defiance to defeat, they win the day-
Stout individualists like these who swing
Back through the storm, on proud disdainful wing.

WHERE LOVERS WALK

There is a place where lovers walk,
A towpath by the winding shore,
Beneath straight cliffs as white as chalk,
Where herons nest and seagulls soar.

Here lovers stroll and never see
The foam of surf the rollers make,
Nor note the small sandpipers flee
Like tumbleweeds when combers break.

They never hear the pounding seas
Nor note the querulous mews of gulls,
For lovers only hear love's pleas,
And why should they see tanker hulls.

Beyond, the alien seascape lies,
But there is nothing to their choice
Except the pageant in Love's eyes,
And golden trumpets in his voice.

There is a place where lovers walk
Though why they walk there puzzles me,
Since they never hear the green tides rock,
Nor look down at the running sea.

I COULD NOT SEE

I could not see before because of thee,
And not that sightless eyes made vision done,
But that thy supple figure hid the sun;
Thy hands eclipsed the moon, and there could be
Naught else beyond thy lips' rose symmetry,
But dull and passionless oblivion;
All beauty merged in thee, becoming one,
And in thee was delight. The alchemy
Of adoration burning to fool's gold,
The warm, soft flesh made from a living maid
A goddess spring, aloof and strangely cold,
To whom I, in my self-abasement prayed,
Now thou art gone, and foolish love is slain,
I see once more but through a mist of pain.

WHEN CHILDREN ARE ABED

The world is such a different place,
When children are abed;
The stars are in a pit of space,
Inverted overhead,
And other stars are large and round,
And set on posts above the ground.

The daytime sky is blue and far,
With momentary floss;
The midnight hangs a silver bar
Of winking stars across.
And where the white sun rolled at noon,
Is now an ogrish-looking moon.

The lamplight on the pavement shines,
And blurs of shadows lie
In angled walls, where stealthy lines
Of timid ghosts go by,
And all is still, as still can be,
Until the wind creeps in from the sea.

And even it would rather stay
Secure on some bare hill,
Than steal along this silent way,
With shadows lying still,
Or weaving shapes, grotesque and strange,
Within the incandescent's range.

Then men who hide from honest gaze,
Prowl the deserted streets,
And some seek gloomy entryways,
For transient safe retreat,
And some, whose weary feet would stay,
In aimless ambit wend their way.

And every footstep cracks the night,
And shapes it to a fear,
And every sound becomes a blight,
That, slinkingly draws near,
And black cats, wild as witches' brew,
Climb up the sill to look at you.

For all is ominous at night,
And tenantless, the town,
Except where wayfarers take flight,
And ghosts go up and down,
Then children should be tucked in bed,
As soon as evening prayers are said.

For night is full of fearsome things,
And shapes are all around,
And horned owls and bats with wings
Rise from the shrouded ground.
In predatory quest they fly,
And make a smudge against the sky.

So, children, when the dark drops down
Kneel by your bed and pray,
And sleep with the good, sleeping town,
And wake with lovely day,
When merry voices will ring out,
And happy children run about.

CONFIGURATION

There have been stars that burned their way across
A moonless sky,
Long, long ere we were born, and that shall toss
Their thin, pale filaments of light
Without a sense of loss
When we shall die.

There have been worlds and ways and men and love,
Ere we were made
That shall go on, Beloved, regardless of
The tragic years that burden with new height
The cypress tree above
Where we are laid.

To you alone am I distinctly drawn,
And you to me.
We are not necessary to the dawn,
Nor does the white moon need us, yet the night
That you are gone, I too shall cease to be.

IF SHE WERE KIND

I had not known of love until today,
Nor did I know its pain could be like this-
An aching stir; a reaching out for bliss,
That, with estranging presence, draws away.

Far better the atrophied pulse of age,
Or callow calm that unawakened lies,
To this pained seeking for a lover's eyes-
Nostalgic hunger nothing can assuage.

Love makes too great a tumult in the soul;
This fret of heart, too ruthless is for peace;
So I would have you go, or staying, cease,
This importuning for a light-flung dole.

If she were kind, Love, I would have you stay,
And would she yield the stiffness of her pride
And come surrendering sweetly to my side,
I could not bear to have you go away.

But now I cannot bear to have you near,
To pluck the tortured strings that sing her name,
And light white flares that blazon out my shame
In holding one who scorns me flower-dear.

LOTH TO GO

It must be hard, the year at its rebirth,
To lay the unwilling body in the tomb,
To turn forever from the lovely earth,
For dark interment in a narrow room.

The unbelieving must be loth to go
When hill winds pick the strings of larkspur lyres;
When monkshood blue is in the dells below;
And slopes flash back the scarlet pimperel fires.

When margined brooks are pricked with iris stalks,
And meadows overflow with poppy gold,
It must be drear to follow where death walks,
To sepulchre in winding sheets of cold.

It must be drear if one has no belief
Or hope in any future beyond death,
But what beatitude and blessed relief,
To one surrendering the fitful breath.

To wake in wide and unexpected fields
With flowers more golden than the vision knew
In Aprils past, and when his spirit kneels
In grateful wonder, drinking in the dew

Of life eternal in this lovely place,
What recompence for faith and hopes deferred;
What gratitude that he was led by grace
And loving, followed Him who is the Word!

KINSHIP

Sometimes one walks ahead with just a hint
Of my lost sweetheart's grace,
And somehow like a palimpsestic print
I see her face.

Again, quiescent night is subtly stirred
By some exotic song,
And suddenly her lovely voice is heard,
Mute overlong.

Sometimes a quick glance out of stranger eyes,
So like to hers,
In darkling depths where sorrow never dies,
New sorrow stirs.

It may be that a look of mine, a phrase,
Becomes a dart
To wound with far intoxicating days
Some other heart.

DIVERGENCE

You were content to let the past slip by,
Like gales beneath the mallard's beating wings,
Your hurried passing aiding them while I
Looked ever wishful back on vanished springs.

I could not let them go. Too precious far,
Where these unshadowed hours for eclipse.
While you were ever traveling towards a star,
I never ceased to hunger for your lips.

WHEN WE PART

When we part,
I shall have naught
But thought
To hold against my heart.

I shall not mind-
For even so
I know
Your thoughts are kind.

So I shall hold
You close, as now,
And vow
The constancy of old.

And I shall think
Of none but you,
And woo
No other fount from whence to drink.

And I shall give
No tiny thought
To aught
But learning how to live.

Without you, Sweet,
Until the day
Your way
And mine shall meet.

ONE WORLD TO SAVE!

Upon the roofs of Bethlehem
Blue moonlight lies,
And twinkling universes gem
Remotest skies,
And placidly exploring them,
A baby's eyes.

A babe within the khan's low shed
In swaddling bands,
Sees how the worlds spin overhead,
And lifts His hands
Above the straw-strewn manger bed
To touch the wheeling lands.

One world alone to save! His care
Broods over all,
And Love, born in a stable bare,
Within a stall
Sees gaunt and dark and sinister,
A gibbet's shadow fall.

And should a million crosses stain
The milky sky
Lest all those worlds in sin remain,
Or darkness lie,
Love would be born anew to pain,
And many times would die.

TODAY, MEN BUILD

Today, men build. They build for other gods,
But not for me.
On marble altar places, Mammon nods
Voluptuously;
And full-paunched Commerce, vulpine-minded Greed
Both fraternize
In every Ziggurat, and flaunt their creed
Of fraud and lies.

Great shrines for trade are tenanted with pride,
And rocket higher
And on the priceless marquetry inside,
Agent and Buyer
Go on to recessed niches whence they bid
And deal and trade;
These are the shrines wherein their gods are hid,
Their altars laid.

Today, men build. Not as in other days,
In wood and stone,
Basilicas where nations came to praise
My Name alone,
Or great cathedral buttresses that hurled
Aloft, gold spires.
Today, corruption in an unchaste world
Lays altar fires.

Before these monstrous, bloated forms which chance
Has shaped for them
From the cupidity of circumstance,
And naught can stem
The columned tides that soar like spray above
An unclean sea.
Today, men build. They build for other gods,
But not for Me.

MY HAND UPON THE PLOW

You will not summon me, Lord, while the task
To which You set my hand is still undone.
Beyond this favor, nothing more I ask,
So help me have a generous harvest run.
You gave these precious souls to me to tend,
And they will need my care a little while,
For there are evil winds that tear and rend
And there are things that touch but to defile.

Without my help they may be forced to yield,
Before they have grown strong enough to stand;
Let me be near to cultivate the field;
To make them ready for the Father's land.
For You have set my hand upon the plough,
I pray You, Lord, do not withdraw it now.

THE MELANCHOLY LAND

Are the jackels still howling for Sharon's sweet rose,
That was broken on Gehon? When the thin Kedron goes
Through the craggy ravine that drops down from the plain
Does it give up its waters because Christ is slain?

Are the cedar and stones of the temple laid low,
And does Rachel's kin weep for the storm winds that blow,
Through the time-ravished courts of the once holy place,
That is roofless because Death lay white on His Face?

Do the tents of Issacher stand tenantless now,
That the dwellers may stand upon Orphels's high brow
As they look for a sign in the cloud tortured sky,
That will tell them the reason the Mighty must die?

Does the harp that was David's make moan in the night,
When the chill winds sweep down from Golgotha's dread height
And the veil that was rent hang its silken shreds o'er
The Holy of Holies' once sancrosanct door?

Has the land been made waste by the anger of God
And the feet of the conqueror bruised the fair sod,
That the country is sterile, and sullen and wild,
And Job's well is dry and silo defiled?

Ah, yes, there is weeping beside Jericho,
And the wailing wall stands as the center of woe,
And the jackels go howling and Rachel's kin cries,
Because the Lord God on a tall gibbet dies.

PLEASURE'S ALLURING LORELEI

Pleasure's wanton Lorelei is flinging
Upon the winds of life, her tarnished hair,
And the sensuous sweet cadence of her singing
Is brightest lure to draw me in its snare.
Should I from this safe ledge go rashly springing,
I would be just one more to perish there.

How many foolish ones before have listened
To lyric measures as I list today,
And while her locks bewilderingly glistened
With seeping sun and chance-caught prismed spray,
Their reckless bodies flashed, and they were christened
By tides that bore them on their final way.

How many more will stand tomorrow, yearning
For this false fair whose song is death to hear,
And tomorrow's morrow, countless others burning,
With bulking thirst will find destruction near,
In darkling depths whence there is no returning,
Nor any hope beyond the sudden bier.

Shall I become as these, as rash, unseeing,
Who answer to desire's insistent surge,
Or shall I flee from this enchanting being
Whose fatal song blends with the river's dirge
The cratered whirlpool waits the soul's betraying,
And pleasure's song is an alluring urge.

THEY DROVE GOD FROM THEIR HEARTS
AND FROM THEIR ALTARS

In some far place and some forgotten moment,
A lovely thing took sudden, wistful flight,
And left an empty space where thought would foment
Excitement to a fever pitch tonight.

I press back through the years behind their boardings
To see if in the debris I can find
Just what it was but there are only hoardings
Of doubtful origin within my mind.

But naught to give a clue to that which presses
Upon my memory to make me yearn
For something - what? Beyond a maid's caresses,
Beyond desires that leap or hopes that burn.

Just what is it, so vague, yet so insistant
That somewhere seemed a splendor and a flame,
My mind, so learning-proud, till now resistant,
Is groping to recall a sacred Name.

And trembling at a wafer moon suspended,
Against the night as though by hands held high,
Somewhere was beauty and that beauty ended,
And there's a torment in me - wondering why.

WATER DROPS

Where go the raindrops, the running again drops,
That drip from the wet shining eaves.
Dripping and slipping and endlessly stripping
The covert of cluttered up leaves.
The basement's loose shutter and furled awnings sputter
And flap when the westerly blows,
But slapping and tapping with ceaseless whip-snapping,
The rain on the gambrel roof goes,
And up in the attic, insistently static,
It hammers with vulcan-like blows.

In the west gable gutters, the downpouring sputters,
And utters its banshee-like wails,
And the tinny rainspout lets the overflow out,
To fill up the great corner pails.
On the oriels rubbing, the drubbing and scrubbing
Goes timelessly into the night,
And the dormers and stormers are thick with reformers,
That are washing them quite out of sight.
But dropping and slopping without any stopping,
The raindrops continue to smite.

The clapboards are harried; the onrush is carried
Like smelted ore down from the roofs;
The overlaps leaping; the cornice is weeping,
And thousands of delicate hoofs
Are whaling and flailing the balcony railing,
Responsive to every fresh goad,
And cloud scuds are bearing to eastward, uncaring,
Just where they deposit their load,
So foaming and combing, torrentially roaming,
They storm down the debris-jammed road.

Till the volume is worsting the mains unto bursting,
And the overworked sewers are flooding
And the walks disappearing beneath the veneering
Of vomited gusts that are scudding
Along on the pavement propulsively forced by
The wind and the smiting of rain,
And driving and driven and merging and riven
The flood waters spread to the plain,
Till spinning and thinning they seek their beginning
To do it all over again.

CHILDBED

We who are born for childbed should not dread
This thing called Death, for death is life at waking-
Each is the shuttle where the weaving thread
Must follow God's design before its breaking.

And we who are His handmaids in the task,
Slow-moving to Life's vestibule of pain,
In solitary travail should not ask
An anasthesia when that Time is slain.

For Birth and Dissolution are the same,
A struggle to draw breath in newer spheres:
For each a momentary poignant flame
Of agony before the change appears.

We women born to travail know of Death
When we slip down the interludes of space,
And so we fear not that insistent breath
That blows the spirit from its prison place.

I CAN SING NO MORE

Now I can sing no more. I have been banished
From gardens where the lovely muses keep,
And memories of epic glories vanished
Leave me with scarcely voice enough to weep.

In one white moment I had thought to enter,
And my earth-heavy feet had found the way,
Through an unguarded portal, but no mentor
Walked at my side on paths where I would stray.

Still I sang on for everywhere was singing,
Until a rose-robed priestess bade me go,
And worshippers with golden censers swinging,
Barred me with scorn as they would blight a foe.

So turned I, disillusioned, discontented,
And heavy with the mocking laughs they hurled,
And ever since I burn and am tormented
With memories of that forbidden world.

And I can sing no more. Unasked, unwanted,
I trespassed fields where I did not belong,
Ungifted soul, and since then I am haunted
With visions of that magic land of song.

ASPASIA

Did this same moon look down on you, Aspasia,
The way it seeks tonight my window space,
And peeps through bars of melon-sweet acacia,
To turn its searchlight on my brooding face.

Is it nostalgic urge that sends it building
Its bridges on the world to find once more
The face that its inimitable gilding
Made men desire and Pericles adore.

At pause, arrested, searching for lost splendor,
It gropes, a lone haunt on a voiceless quest
Into the gloom, where, like the witch of Endor,
I brew sad thoughts in smoldering unrest.

And wan from fruitless journeyings, it lingers
As though, it, hoping against hope may find
Herein, the golden maid, and its cool fingers,
Are troubling me like fingers of the blind.

And does it sigh as it renews its seeking,
To build its bridges new, and swing its arcs,
Pearl-luster in the night, while it goes peeking
Forever in dim rooms and shadowed parks.

PATHWAYS

There's naught but rumpled petals of lost pleasures
Along the path that you would have me go,
And I would gather no enduring treasures,
As those who dance along its stardust know.

This way of mine is narrow-laid and lonely,
Full-straight ahead with no intriguing bend;
I would prefer your joyous pathways, only,
There are too many heartaches at the end.

WINDOWS

Wide windows framed your splendid youth so often
When I have stopped my work to watch you play,
What will there be, my little son, to soften
This grief of mine, when I look out today!

Long windows held you in their clean embrasure,
Since your unsteady steps went out of doors,
How can I stand the unforeseen erasure
Of boyhood doing his appointed chores.

Void shining glass where vision dully lingers,
With wistful hope and unexpected tears,
Clean sponged of smudges made by little fingers
And empty of the merriment of years.

WHEN LOVE AND HOPE HAVE LEFT

The soul cries out for some substantial thing
To which in utter loneliness to cling,
For nothing in all nature is bereft
As is the soul when love and hope have left
It tries to find a substitute for each
And finds instead that they are out of reach-
The things for which it gropes, and so despair
Follows the dark into the nether air.

How foolishly it yearned for what it sought-
How futily it seeks for what is not;
And empty are the dreams that it has bought.
For nothing can replace what it has lost
Unless it seeks again the wave, star-crossed
Where love and hope was once so blithely tossed.

NOW IS THE ACCEPTABLE TIME

Heart of Mine! Heart of Mine! Bear with your sorrow;
Pain of the parting and terror of loss.
These are the splinters that each soul must borrow
From the dark wood that must fashion his cross-
These are the splinters with which he must build it,
Out of his heart's blood and wet with his tears;
There was another, and Sorrow had milled it-
Gaunt has its shadow hung over the years;
Long has its shadow been moulding the years.

There was Another who hung dead upon it;
Spiked like a pelt that a huntsman had dried,
After the chase with the blood clotted on it.
Was there a reason this Other had died?
Yes, Heart of Mine, that when your time for grieving,
Came with the years you would not grieve alone.
For this has He suffered beyond all believing-
For this has He hung on his high, cruel throne.
Hung like a thief on His cruel high throne.

Heart of Mine! Heart of Mine! Suffer your anguish.
Bear with the torment of fear and desire.
See how the White Christ in dolour must languish;
Wounds gaping red and His veins running fire.
What can you suffer that was not His portion?
Pain, desolation, desertion and fear-
All were exacted by Love's mad extortion-
All yielded up on His terrible bier.
Yielded by Him on His heart-breaking bier.

Heart of Mine! Heart of mine cannot console you.
Only His heart holds the solace you need.
Only His love has the power to hold you
Close to the cross if your soul will but heed.

Here is new strength flowing out from the Dying;
The peace that you long for so desperately now;
The Covenant signed where His heart's blood is drying,
With the seal of the Promise upon His pierced brow-
Starred in red letters upon His pale brow.

Heart of Mine! Heart of Mine! Here is the answer
To your bewilderment; to your soul's ache-
Sorrow eats into your heart like a cancer,
Because you forget that He died for your sake.
To "Fill up the things that are wanting," you suffer,
The price of your peace is His blood and your tears.
Oh Heart that goes sorrowing on roads growing rougher,
Consider how short are these sorrowful years-
How short and acceptable are these few years.

UNCOMPANIONED

If you should come back once could I be gay,
With all the old abandon of the past,
Would you make prose again the formal way
That I have traveled since I saw you last.

Or would you, startled, meet the eyes you knew
With the old sweet divinatory gaze
That dominates each memory of you
And makes distrait my thoughts and frets my days.

I could forget you but for your young eyes
That played upon my soul too long for peace,
I pray you come back once and exorcize
The lone lost spirit weeping for release.

SHASTA

Cool, calm majestic Shasta, etched in white,
Upon the periwinkle sky of June,
Sharp as a polar vista traced in light
Thin arctic contours on somnolent noon,
Etherialized, eternal pyramid,
Carved with its glacial fingertips of snow,
Like a pearl shadow earthly moorings hid,
By mist scarves flung down flutteringly below.

I have seen nothing so exquisitely
Detached and mystical, so hung in space
Against the sky as in a polar sea,
Still-dreaming argent beauty, recessed grace,
And weightless whiteness, textured like a cloud,
Classic, introspectional, alone;
Surpliced in pascal snow, and virginal-browed;
A vestal at the Great White Spirit's throne.

BLUE AND SILVER

Was it on such a blue and silver day,
They took His life away?

How could they think of death with April there,
And sunshine everywhere!

When hills loomed blue beyond Jerusalem,
And every wayside stem,

By showers refreshed, still held the shining rain,
And every lovely lane

Was burgeoning with promise, how could they
Lift angry hands to slay.

When clouds in mobile beauty came and went,
Across a firmament,

Deep-tinctured with the dawn, did they arise,
With hate-averted eyes,

And hearts of bitterness that deigned no look
At Kedron's wrinkled brook,

Out side the walls. If they had stopped to gaze
And hear sweet April's praise,

Would they not know that in the ribald ring
Of persecutors stood Creation's King.

And would they not in adoration feel
The holy urge to kneel.

Instead of slay, and feeling, understand
That all the quickening land

Would mourn if death should touch that sacred Brow.
Oh, foolish Ones, stop now,

Ere that is done that would be Nature's stain.
Mark not the brand of Cain

Upon a world that sheds its Brother's blood.
Stem now the Precious Flood

That drops upon the earth ere April dies,
With deep and wounded Cries.

FALLING

An inner voice that is a part
Of me, though soft and small,
Beats at the portals of my heart,
When meteors blaze and fall.

Does it perchance, remember when
The angels, sinning fell,
And dropped beyond the planet's ken,
Like brands to fire hell.

It moans when leaves drop recklessly,
In tired broken moans,
And when a gull dips in the sea,
Despairfully, it groans.

It whimpers when the snow sifts down,
A plaintive, baby sound,
And sobs when rain beats on the town,
And runs along the ground.

It is as though it shudders when
Things fall from overhead,
If it but knew they rose again,
Would it be comforted.

Then, hush, Small Voice, that cries and cries,
Leaves drop and then decay,
That from rich loam strong trees may rise,
To grace another day.

The snowflakes gurgle into rills,
And rush to join the sea,
And rains that pour upon the hills,
Will join them presently.

So cease complaining, Little Voice,
Because the sky sheds tears,
For nature has no other choice
To propagate the years.

The rhythmic flow ebb-tide and flood,
And so life carries on;
The lifted cross, the drip of blood,
The dark and then the dawn.

Down, Flesh, to earth; Up, Spirit, rise,
The tragic hour is past.
Hush, Little Voice, that cries and cries,
Be comforted at last.

LIVING THINGS MUST GROW

Today he went in childish pride to school,
Without a backward look,
And left me here, and boldly went with rule,
And pad and book.

And I am sad because my baby son
Has grown to boy's estate,
The hours of my dictatorship are done,
And I must abdicate.

The empire of the home is narrow ground,
For sons to thrive and grow,
For love would only compass them around
When there is much to know.

So gladly, if reluctantly, I see
My little one depart,
Because I know that none can take from me
His loyal little heart.

JOY OF FLIGHT

I try to lift myself above
This couch where health was slain,
But I have need of wings of Love
To rise above my pain.

I cannot raise my heavy length
Without the aid of prayer,
Or pinions of a seagull's strength,
So valiant in the air.

So I must lie upon my bed,
While stronger souls arise,
With sweeping flight and mighty spread
Of wing tips in the skies.

So, Helpless, I, while others go
Along the holy way.
Oh help me, Lord, that I may know
The joy of flight today.

AUGUST DAYS

These are the warm and glowing days,
When shimmering rays
Are marshalling along the valley line;
And Blossoms like a sumac blaze
Are rippling in the blue heat haze,
Like tapers seen through incense smoke,
Before Our Lady's shrine.

The sky, Our Lady's mantle-blue
Holds but a few
If any clouds that tell of change to be;
Except a baby cloud or two,
May come like cherubs into view,
And hover like the angels hover
At Our Lady's knee.

An interregnum, seen the days;
A passing phase;
A pause where one may meditate and grow;
A time of prayer; a time of praise;
Of sober thoughts and sober ways;
An interval for questioning,
And pulses running slow.

This is the healing interlude;
The calm prelude
Of harvestings to come and precious yields;
A time of blessed certitude
That presages beatitude
For countless little souls that grow
Within the Father's fields.

These are the days of peace and prayer;
Of holy and reposeful air,
When doubts are gently stilled and hopes are stirred;
When those who dwell upon His care
May, with His Blessed Mother, share
The glory of His Being, and
The Promise of His Word.

A SINGER OF SONGS

He finds his lovely words
But not where smugness keeps its studded doors
Barred tight on novel thoughts, like student birds
That, having learned their scores,
Repeat them, faultlessly and endlessly and sweet

He goes beyond the bars
Of wind and cloud and air,
Out where the farthest stars
Fling burning meteors down, like rocket flares,
And these,
He uses for his superb harmonies.

A courier of space, he ranges wide
In that far place
Where planets, multiplied,
Swing in great arcs about a glowing sun,
And from the furnace sparks
He forges one,
Two, three, a score
Of syllables of fire,
And words that pour
In meters of desire.

A comet passes
With its streaming mane
Of fiery gases, on the starry plain;
He gathers motes of these to shape an ode,
And, earthward floats
With his ethereal load,
And, having tied his winged horse to the ground,
He flings them wide
In lovely flakes of sound.

YOUTH HAS NO FEAR

Sometimes we youthful ones decide that we
Are bravely ready to face life alone,
Forgetting that man acted foolishly
In other days when he was on his own.
Youth has no fears because it does not know
The pitfalls of the future and the snares
That life can throw before him unawares
Along the road that he would blithely go.

Youth has to try its wings but he is wise
Who charts his course more carefully than most
Who takes close cognizance of threatening skies
And prideful in success restrains his boast.
Who seeks good counsel and with reverence heeds
The words that wisdom offers to his needs.

WHERE LOVE ABIDES

My thanks, Dear God, for this sweet House of Grace.
And blessed certainty of Love abiding;
That, immolated on the altar place
Divinest glory for the soul's confiding
Is regnant Host, who deigns not to appear
But hides behind the sacramental veil;
Encompassing the world, He chooses here
To hold His court within the Holy Grail.

As truly present as in that far room,
Where chosen ones beheld Him breaking bread;
The sanctuary lamp burns through the gloom,
And seeing, I am strangely comforted.
The tapers near the tabernacle flare,
And glint upon the tiny golden key,
That locks Him in, and knowing He is there,
I am content, and sit adoringly.

Content to sit without a prayer or sigh;
To find refreshment, just in being near,
Oh, Lord, what matters it to live or die,
Since all the sweets of heaven are centered here.
And all that makes of heaven a Paradise,
Is circumscribed within this hallowed spot.
Here I renounce the worldling's foolish prize.
Content to be by all the world forgot.

THE WEDDING FEAST

The golden cup now holds the ruby wine
But it must go to other lips than mine.
I drank to love once long ago but now
I cannot drink for love has failed somehow.

And I could only drink to memories
Out of a wooden cup that holds the lees
Left from a vintage wine of long ago,
When music throbbed and guests went to and fro

Tasting the wedding cake and drinking toasts
To bride and bridegroom who today are ghosts
At other wedding feasts and cannot drink
To bridal happiness because they shrink

From all the pains of knowledge for they fear
A happiness that lasts but for a year
Then leaves a trail of anguish in its wake
And hearts that know how other hearts can break.

The golden cup that holds the ruby wine
Is meant for us to drink whose days decline
To golden sunset years - two hearts whose thoughts
Have grown together as for-get-me-nots

Upon one spray - small, delicate and sweet
They dwell upon each other, each complete
Only when shared. And now today we two
Drink to each other and to the years we knew.

These were not perfect years - How could they be!
When two were made to share one destiny
Each had to yield some portion of his side
And bit by stubborn bit renounce his pride.

But we held on to love and day by day
We found the going peaceful and the way
Became more beautiful as time passed on
And now those golden years are almost gone,

But while they last together we will go
Into the sunset years with hearts that know
The future promises more than did the past,
Because we know true love will always last.

ANTITHETICAL

There are some things that you may never know,
That stir me as the tolling of a bell,
You who are practical and sure to go
Along frequented ways where you must dwell,

But which would prove an agony to feet
Unused to aught but needle-paths of woods;
That crush the eucalyptus burrs and beat
So joyously through cedar solitudes.

For me are torches in the forest paths;
Flame tapers where my soul perforce must kneel;
While you take cognizance of beams and laths,
And structural things, cold riveted with steel.

Oh, yes, I know that you burn with desires,
But I could have no part of their white flame.
Ambition could not stir me with its fires -
I would be as I was before you came.

AFTERMATH

Could I but see you once again, I wonder
Would all the quivering pain of loss be still;
I think that nerves torn ruthlessly asunder
Are always ill.

And being stretched and wrenched so is it reason
That they should feel the past urbanities.
By weakness shamed, and broken by their treason,
They flee old vanities.

So should you come it would not matter greatly,
If pain would go - if nerves be ill or well,
Apostate to desires, I have learned lately
Serenity's sweet spell.

So I can look within on pain and wonder
That life goes on despite this querulous ache,
So should my love again be trampled under,
What difference would it make.

A DAY LIKE THIS

A day like this brings back too much to bear,
For strangled thoughts writhe to remembered breath,
And with returning consciousness, I dare
Not let them live lest they bring back the death

I suffered long ago. For there is more
Than this one death whereby the body dies.
That Death is but the opening of the door
That lets the spirit in to Paradise.

There is a Death that, shutting out all hope,
Becomes a watch beside a buried tomb,
And on a day like this, blind fingers grope
To snatch me back within the mourning room.

The breeze that lifts my hair is a caress
From that far past that must have fluttered by
In moments of remembered happiness,
And being stored with sweets was loth to die.

The bundle clouds that are like triumphs pass;
The foothills lift green billows to their spray;
The world of sky and water is, alas!
As shining as before you went away.

And peace would flow from these, and wounded heart
Would lie within the comfort of its breast,
Did not this breeze that should remain apart,
Come torturing with hopes long dispossessed.

CONTRAST

The evergreens are robed in rich
And festal clothes that set them well,
The naked maples writhe and pitch
To tearing winds, like souls in Hell.

My body feels the kiss of furs,
Wears vesture soft and silken warm;
Soliciting from almoners,
A beggar beats against the storm.

DECADENCE

The muse who kept her shrine within
The temple of my mind,
Has gone away to other kin,
And left me dumb and blind.

Her altar fires untended are,
Her marble throne forlorn,
The incense smoke has spiraled far,
The arras screens are torn.

Rich samite cloths are threadbare too,
And vandals have destroyed
The faultless pictures that she drew,
And left the temple void.

No pomp nor glory to delight;
No manuscript nor scroll;
No beauty to make glad the sight;
No worship for the soul.

An empty shrine is this I keep,
Without a single grace,
So how can I do aught but weep,
In this deserted place.

THIS LOVING HURTS

This loving hurts.
It may be that in loving so
One reaches heights or plumbs to depths,
That only the untimid know,
Abysmal with unmeasured woe.

It may be that in loving thus,
The hilltop winds blow down to us,
To soothe the ache that knowledge brings
That time and life and love have wings,
And all so brief,
With just around the corner, grief.

It may be that in loving much,
One feels the chilling mistral touch
Of that hard day that has to be,
Disintegrating entity
When two who thought so long as one,
Must in divergent orbits run.

It may be, loving now, today,
One borrows love and so must pay
The interest on the loan in tears,
Since one would compass into years'
Short finite span that which was meant
To be eternal sacrament.

SECOND STORY BACK

My dreams today would fashion a boudoir
Of simple loveliness, the luxury
Of speckless beauty. There would be a door
Of mullionod glass, undraped; French ivory
Would be the motif for the bedroom set,
Spread with a cluny bordered marquisette;
A hooked rug would be on the oaken floor;
A pillow top or two, and nothing more.

Except the clean transparency of panes,
Filmed with flock-dotted voile with ruffled edge,
And tie-backs, so that I could see the lanes
Of garden blooms along the privet hedge;
And closer, where the patio becalms,
The mingled wings of two great cocoa palms,
With shadows smudging the encroaching sky,
Where thornbills dart and crested beauties fly.

Beyond them, there would be a somber spar-
A Norfolk-Island pine, correctly boughed;
A eucalyptus, drooping to the far
Horizon, veiled in distance and a cloud.
Here, I would find appeasement for life's ills,
A respite from its ever-hounding chores;
A sanctuary that sweet quiet fills;
A flowering vista of the out-of-doors.

IMMEASURABLY SWEET

That love is but a word, I'll not believe,
For Love once died to show that Love still lived,
And out through all its pores His blood was sieved
And lay upon the world. So could I grieve
Because there is no love when this I know
With all my being, that love is a part
Of that great longing palpitating heart
That shuddered at mankind's remembered woe.

Oh foolish heart that would dissemble so,
And mouth the ancient lies to make us feel
Alone in life and bound to its grim wheel,
When love is all around us who can go
Unfathomable distances to meet
A waiting love immeasurably sweet.

FIRST LINES

Today, men build. They build for other gods,   20

You will not summon me, Lord, while the task   21

Are the jackels still howling for Sharon's sweet rose,   22

Pleasure's wanton Lorelei is flinging   23

In some far place and some forgotten moment,   24

Where go the raindrops, the running again drops,   25

We who are born for childbed should not dread   27

Now I can sing no more. I have been banished   28

Did this same moon look down on you, Aspasia,   29

There's naught but rumpled petals of lost pleasures   30

Wide windows framed your splendid youth so often   31

The soul cries out for some substantial thing   32

Heart of Mine! Heart of Mine! Bear with your sorrow;   33

If you should come back once could I be gay,   35

Cool, calm majestic Shasta, etched in white,   36

Was it on such a blue and silver day,   37

An inner voice that is a part   39

Today he went in childish pride to school,   41